Also by Tom Molnar

Time Out for Happiness

Jesus, Kind, Loving, Dangerous

The Universe of God and Humanity

Mary, the Girl Who Said Yes

Wired for Love

The Crisis of Christianity

Fiction

Swept Away

Dark Age Maiden

Mist on the Moon

The Joys of Science and Religion

By

Tom Molnar

Apple Valley Press

The Wonders of Science and Religion

Copyright 2024 ©

ISBN 978-1-7343593-6-7

Manufactured in the United States of America.

Apple Valley Press

The Joys of Science and Religion

Today, most of us profess faith in God, yet in everyday life we are surrounded by science. Our cars, phones, TV's and even the heating and cooling of our homes is all thanks to science.

However, we ourselves are not scientific beings. We are totally human, trying to live the best life we can in today's world. Life can be difficult. Fortunately, both science and faith can come to our aid. This book looks at the realities of our times, as well as our religious heritage, to show how they can help or hinder us to make the most of our life on earth.

Chapters

Note: This book follows a pattern with a number of topics. The first chapters tell the important story of what happened leading to modern times. Then, the focus is on today's times and how they impact our lives. The heading at the start of each chapter describes it.

Forward

Long before recorded human history, men and women were making discoveries and inventing things to make life easier. Similarly, archeological evidence from ancient times shows an abiding interest in spiritual matters and life after death. Archeologists posit different estimates on how long mankind lived on the earth before developing systems of writing. However, it has been determined that more than a million years ago sharp hand axes were fashioned by human ancestors and used to cut meat and vegetables. Also, not long afterwards, fire was utilized at home sites for cooking and for warmth.

A very significant discovery relating to making clothing was the invention of the sewing needle. Many sewing needles made of bone with a sharp point on one side and an eye at the other have been found dating from about 50,000 BC. Other important inventions, long before recorded history, include making pottery for dishes and jugs for water storage as well as crafting boats and then sail boats. Art is well represented by the dramatic and colorful cave paintings made as long as 40,000 years ago that can still be seen in France, Spain,

Mexico and other countries. Early humans long ago must have sung melodies, and flutes from the Neanderthal period over 50,000 years ago and later in Germany dating from 35,000 BCE give physical evidence to the human love of music.

As for religion, long before recorded history human grave sites often included objects of life. The significant articles buried with the dead, including pottery, tools and even food seems to show belief in an afterlife. In historic times the ancient Babylonian and Egyptian religions are both polytheistic, that is having belief in many gods. This is true for the premodern Indian tribes of North America as well as for the remaining native peoples of Africa. The belief in many gods continued in Greece and then in the Roman Empire during much of its history. Their polytheistic belief was largely supplanted by Christianity in the fourth century AD.

From Many Gods to One

This chapter shows the remarkable transition of the Roman Empire from a country worshiping many gods and severely persecuting Christians to a land that adopted the religion of Christ.

The earliest historical civilizations, Sumerian, Greek, Egyptian, and Roman, all had great numbers of gods. In the eighth century BC when Rome began as an agricultural society, religion was animistic with the belief that everything in the world had a soul including common things like mountains, thunder, water, etc. Then, by the time the first Christians arrived in the Roman Empire in the first century AD, Rome had a panoply of gods and goddesses. Many of them they had imported from Greece, a country they had defeated in 146 BC.

The Romans seem to have had gods for almost everything, but their major gods were the powerful Jupiter, protector of the state, Juno, protector of women, and Minerva, goddess of craft and wisdom. Other major gods include Mars, the god of war, Mercury, god of trade and messages, Bacchus, the god of grapes and wine, Venus, the goddess of love, Neptune, god of the sea and water and Diana, goddess of the hunt. The Roman leaders early on did not mistreat people of other religions, including those who professed Judaism and Christianity. However, many Romans developed some negative ideas about Christianity. They perceived that eating the body and blood of Christ was akin to cannibalism.

The first terrible persecution of Christians did not take place until 64 AD, after the great fire of Rome. The emperor, Nero had petitioned the senate to tear down a major part of the city of Rome so that he could erect palaces and royal gardens adorned with monuments. The senate refused his request and not long afterwards a major fire began that, fed by strong winds, consumed almost two thirds of the districts of Rome. Nero was implicated, and to rebuff accusations he accused Christians of setting the fire.

Christians were rounded up, nailed to crosses, put in animal skins to be torn apart by dogs and burned in the night, their bodies serving as torches to light up Nero's gardens. It was during this time that St. Peter died on a cross, thirty-one years after Christ, upside down as is the tradition. Also, during this same time St. Paul was beheaded. As a Roman citizen from birth Paul could not be crucified.

Nero's life was short. Although his mother, Agrippina, had helped him become emperor at the age of 17 by murdering his rivals, Nero later had her killed, apparently because she wanted to control his actions. He also murdered his first wife and then his second, becoming more and more out of control with his lusts and his desire to be a great performer in the theater. In the end, the Senate declared him a public enemy such that anyone was licensed to kill him. Knowing that troops were on their way to seize him, Nero committed suicide with the aid of a slave. He died at only 30 years of age.

After the Nero inspired persecution of Christians subsided, Christianity continued to grow within the huge territory of the Roman Empire. A number of factors account for its rise. For one, in a polytheist state where numerous gods were the tradition, it was easy for Romans to add one more, Jesus Christ. Second, the message of Jesus with his teaching of love of God and love of neighbor and the promise of an afterlife in paradise may have been comforting to many of the Romans turned off by the carnage of gladiator combat and the crucifixion of slaves. The saints Peter and Paul and others were important in spreading the message of Christianity while they were alive but it is likely that the later dissemination of the faith was carried on person to person.

Another reason for the growth of Christianity in the Roman Empire is less obvious but is well attested to in Rodney Stark's book, *The*

Rise of Christianity. Many Romans practiced infanticide, leaving undesired children out in the elements to die. Boy babies were, for many, more desirable than girls so it was newborn girls who more often suffered this cruel fate. Very often, Christians on finding such a child would rescue them, find a nursing mother to care for them and raise them up in Christian families. The result was that in time there were more young women in the Empire, many of them Christian, than men of marriageable age.

A well known example of this, even in the fourth century AD, is that of Saint Monica who was given in marriage to Patricius, a pagan. After a period of time, she converted her husband to Christianity and finally her famous son, Saint Augustine. St. Augustine was an intellectual who studied the literature and thinking of his day before finally converting to Christianity. His erudition and talent for public speaking was recognized and he soon became a bishop and later a renowned doctor of the Church. Before his conversion Augustine had a thirteen year relationship with a woman whom he obviously loved but who was beneath him in class. Consequently, in that time period he could not marry her. Interestingly, the Church in those days allowed its members in such relationships to attend Mass and receive communion. This was affirmed by the Church Council of Toledo held in 400 AD.

St. Augustine was a great homilist and prolific writer and his works are to this day read by Christians around the world.

In regard to the persecutions against Christians, they were not continuous but instead were sporadic. Although in some parts of the empire local persecutions prevailed, after Nero's time the next major persecution occurred almost 100 years later under Marcus Aurelius who was emperor from 161 to 180 AD. Major subsequent persecutions resumed from 251 through 260 and the particularly heinous persecution under Augustus Diocletian lasted from 283 to 305 AD.

The Romans seem to have had no concept of "cruel and unusual punishment" for Christians were subjected to the most inhumane tortures. Subjection to the rack, crucifixion, feeding to wild animals, burning on grills, etc. were all employed against Christians who refused to offer libations to Roman gods. Many Christians went to their deaths with joy in their strong belief in Christ and their own salvation following their execution. Saint Lawrence, who in 258 AD was grilled to death on a slow fire is reliably recounted to have said, "Turn me over, I'm done on this side!"

Not every Christian had the strength to suffer a painful death. Some complied with the law and poured a small amount of wine into a sacred cup representing a god and, in some cases, even received a certificate for having done so. Those who had done so were called "lapsi" because they had lapsed in their faith. In the interims between persecutions what to do with them caused much dissension within the Church. Some of the Christians, many of those who had suffered imprisonment, said that the lapsi should never be allowed back into the Church. Others remembered that even Saint Peter had denied Christ. Despite all the discussions that went on about the matter, in virtually all cases the lapsi were allowed to return to the Church after receiving absolution.

Finally, in dramatic fashion, the persecutions against Christians ended in the Roman Empire in 312 AD. In a history changing battle that Constantine was to fight against the other Roman emperor, Maxentius, it is reported that Constantine, on the evening of the battle, saw the image of a cross near the sun with the words, "By this sign you will conquer." Though he had a smaller army, Constantine decisively won the battle of Milvian Bridge and thus made himself the single ruling emperor of the Roman Empire. He immediately stopped the persecution of Christians and the following year issued the Edict of Milan making Christianity an officially recognized and tolerated religion.

Christianity had been growing in the Roman Empire notwithstanding the intermittent persecutions. It continued to grow perhaps even more rapidly once it became an officially permitted religion. By 380 AD the Emperor Theodosius made Christianity the official religion of the Roman Empire. With Christianity came a new development: hospitals. A number of influential Christians began to recognize the need for care facilities for the common people. Rome had no hospitals for its citizens although they did have competent doctors to treat the injuries of gladiators and Roman soldiers. It has been written that on average Roman soldiers lived longer than the general populace. Doctors did provide care for those who were wealthy, coming to their homes to administer treatment.

The first hospitals for the general populace began in the eastern half of the Roman Empire in Constantinople, which is in present day Turkey. In Rome itself, the first general hospital was built in the fourth century AD by a wealthy widow, Saint Fabiola. Fabiola is herself an interesting person. Her training and life work was that of a physician. Coming from a family of wealth, she married well but divorced her dissolute husband and then remarried while he was still alive, sinful according to the Church. When her second husband died an early death, Fabiola made a public confession and dedicated her life to serving the sick who were most in need. She personally cared for the most diseased patients. Her influence in caring for the sick continued and after 400 AD the many monasteries that were built throughout Europe generally provided not only care for the sick but also accommodations for travelers. Christian emperors, such as Charlemagne, directed that a hospital should be attached to every cathedral of the empire.

The Rise of Science and Religion

This section discloses the terrible conditions following the fall of Rome that led to a whole new way of life. Feudal kingdoms arose along with monasteries, nunneries and the flowering of knighthood. Some major inventions that we now take for granted were developed and improved during this "Age of Faith."

The Roman Empire had been declining in size and power since late in the third century AD. It's Christianization in the fourth century did nothing to prevent its further decline or the destructive invasions by peoples the Romans called "barbarians." In 476 AD the last Roman emperor, Romulus Augustus, was deposed and his place taken by a Germanic military leader named Odoacer. In most regions the subsequently reduced size of the Roman Empire, things continued as before and even the senators still held positions in Rome. Those Romans living on large landed estates continued to use slaves and others to farm their acreage. However, with the increasing lawlessness that abounded when the military power of Rome was lost, the patricians found it necessary to fortify their residences and erect tall fences around part of their estates. They also hired soldiers to protect their domains.

After the fall of Rome, times were precarious. Lawless bands of fighting men roamed throughout much of the countryside terrorizing the inhabitants and taking what they wanted from farmers and the citizens of small towns and hamlets. Even Rome itself saw its population decline from as many as a million people at its zenith to less than 40,000 people by the seventh century. The rise in death and destruction caused a flight from the towns to the relative safety that could be found on large country estates. In agreements reached with the magistrates of the estates people desperate for protection became essentially sharecroppers of the estate owner. The word feudum is the Roman word for a landed estate and it explains how feudalism came to be the dominant way of life across much of what is today known as Europe.

Despite the breakdown of the old society under Rome, Christianity continued to grow and missionaries were sent to Ireland (St. Patrick) to England, (St. Augustine) [not the St. Augustine of the fourth century] and to Germany, (St. Boniface) among many others. The Roman educational system had broken down and as a result most people during this time were illiterate. However, many monasteries both small and large were founded much along the style of the traditional manorial system throughout much of Europe beginning in the fifth century. In much the same way as life in nonreligious manors, monks performed all the tasks that were essential for day to day life, including farming, animal husbandry, bread baking, wine cultivation, carpentry and blacksmith crafts. They also cultivated plants and herbs known for their medicinal properties. In addition, they maintained high literacy standards for themselves and spent specific times of the day in prayer and devotion.

Monasteries both large and small provided care to aid the sick and dying and tried to nurse those in their care back to health with rest, wholesome food and herbal medications. Larger monasteries even ran schools for nobles and others who would send their male children there for education. Typically, during much of the Middle Ages, women were not educated unless they were wealthy and had private tutoring or if they lived in a convent. Within the monasteries subjects taught were religion, reading and writing Latin, chant and also arithmetic. In time, convents or nunneries for women became quite common as well, the nuns also maintaining themselves by means of agriculture, animal husbandry, cooking and baking. The convents maintained high educational standards for women and in the course of the day set aside specific times for prayer and adoration.

Gradually, monasteries, convents and manors tended to increase in size. Wealthy patrons sometimes gave land to religious communities, and fighting men, soon to be called knights, fought small and large battles to win control over large estates. With power came prestige and wealth, and in time dukes, kings and nobles built impressive castles fortified to withstand all but the most determined and powerful adversaries. By 1000 AD, most of Europe had entered into an era of castle building and eventually tens of thousands of them dotted the countryside. In what subsequently became Germany, Austria, France, England and to a lesser extent Italy, the distance from one castle to the next was likely less than ten miles. Many of the largest of these remain, impressive monuments to a bygone age.

The Middle Ages is also remembered for knights and chivalry. However, it didn't start out that way at all. In the general lawlessness after the fall of Rome, those with military prowess often took what they wanted from defenseless farmers and townspeople. Theft, murder and rape were often unrestrained in major parts of Europe. Some of these brigands were hired by the lords of the manor to protect their landed estates from outside attacks. As payment they received their own land within the area controlled by the manor.

During the time that the manor system and feudalism became the dominant way of life, the church grew in power and influence. In its efforts to protect the powerless, it established a code for men at arms. In time, the induction of men into knighthood became a highly religious ceremony with a ritual bathing, an all-night vigil while garbed in white vesture, and a morning Mass ceremony before finally being dubbed "Sir Knight." As part of the ceremony, the young knight would take an oath to fight against wrong-doers and to protect widows, orphans and the poor.

Recognizing the destructiveness of warfare among the hundreds of petty kingdoms striving for land and power, the Church also instituted the "Truce of God" beginning in 1027 in Southern France which limited the days on which fighting could take place. Initially it forbade hostilities from Saturday night until Monday morning. The Truce gradually spread from France to Italy and Germany and in time fighting was banned during all the days of Advent and Lent. The penalty for initiating hostilities during these proscribed times was excommunication from the Church.

The early and middle part of the Middle Ages has been called "The Age of Faith" and it easy to see why it was so named. The Christian Church, undividedly Catholic at the time, was powerful because it held sway over all the religious activity and belief of both the rich and the poor. Furthermore, the church had a monopoly on literacy such that particularly in the early Middle Ages almost anyone who wanted an education had to go to a monastery or Cathedral school. There, training was provided in any of the subjects that were available, which ordinarily included theology, reading and writing in Latin, and rhetoric (or speech). Other courses that were sometimes taught included logic, arithmetic, geometry, astronomy and music. Even astronomy tended to be suffused with religious values.

Nevertheless, major inventions and discoveries were made during the Middle Ages. One that was very important to the livelihood of people was the invention of the heavy plow sometime during the ninth century. This type of implement allowed farming of the heavier soils present in climes north of Italy. Another invention necessary for the flowering of knighthood was the use of stirrups. Though likely invented in China, it was developed in Europe in the 8th and 9th centuries and was a major factor in the rise of cavalrymen who with stirrups could fight while mounted on their horses while carrying a heavy lance, shield and sword.

People had from ancient times kept track of the approximate time with the use of sundials. Telling time that way was actually taught in monastery schools. Of course, their disadvantage was their uselessness on cloudy days and at night. The hourglass, using fine sand to record time, was also utilized during the Middle Ages with different size glasses allowing for better timekeeping. Then, in 1283 the first weight driven clock was installed at a priory in Dunstable, Bedfordshire, England. By the turn of the century, in 1300 AD, clocks were being built for churches and cathedrals in France and Italy.

An invention that changed history was the development of the printing press. It was originally invented by Pi Sheng, a Chinese alchemist, in 1040 AD. However, the new technology didn't make a great impact in China. A likely reason is that the Chinese language uses thousands of characters. The English language, by comparison, uses only twenty-six letters. Johann Gutenberg's more usable printing press in 1440 made possible the mass production of books and pamphlets and heralded the onset of the High Renaissance in Europe.

Another invention also changed history. It was the invention of gunpowder. First discovered by the Chinese, it began to be used and developed in Europe in the fourteenth century. By the fifteenth and sixteenth century, the development of firearms and cannon using gunpowder made the armor worn by knights useless. Similarly, only the most formidable castle walls were able to withstand cannon fire. Today, gunpowder used in single shot and rapid fire weapons remains a highly destructive force.

Increasing Atheism and Denial of Miracles

In the aftermath of the Renaissance new discoveries showed that the earth is not the center of creation but is only one of many planets that revolve around the sun. The Church fought the finding and many intelligent men, including some well known founders of our country, came to the conclusion that God doesn't care about human beings. Others decided there is no God.

Throughout the Middle Ages the Church was a powerful organization. It retained the Latin language of the Roman empire and kept learning alive through monastery and cathedral schools. Before the advent of the printing press in 1440, monks meticulously made copies of the Bible as well as important Greek and Roman works of literature and science. Monasteries provided care facilities for the sick and the Church also maintained cathedral hospitals where people could receive care and treatment. The Catholic Church played a major role in the Renaissance, and in the flowering of art and learning. The beautiful artistry of the period focused mostly on biblical subjects and themes.

In the late Middle Ages, a number of powerful people sought to limit the dominance of the Church. Whereas the Church had been both religiously and politically a powerful force in the medieval world, new ideas and thinking began to emerge that sought to relegate Christianity to a lesser station. Some of these viewpoints arose following major scientific developments. Two of the most important were the discoveries of Copernicus and Galileo and those of Isaac Newton.

Copernicus came to realize, using mathematical analysis, that planets move around the sun rather than the earth. He determined that the sun is the center of the solar system. Like most people of the time, Copernicus was a member of the Church. Galileo, who followed him years later verified his findings, and using one of the first telescopes, determined visually that the sun, not the earth was the center of the solar system. Galileo was also a practicing Catholic whose two daughters became nuns.

Unfortunately, the Catholic Church was powerful enough at the time to declare that heliocentrism, the earth moving around the sun, was irreligious, based on psalm nineteen and other parts of the Bible. Consequently, Galileo was brought to court in Rome and in 1633 was sentenced to house arrest. There, for the next nine years Galileo lived in his own house. He was able to receive guests, including some distinguished people of his time, and to write his book, *Two New Sciences*. Because it would have been banned in Italy, it was published in Holland. The book received acclaim in its day and centuries later was highly praised even by Albert Einstein. Eventually, 359 years later, in 1992 Pope John Paul II admitted that Galileo was right and the Catholic Church was wrong in condemning him.

Galileo's discovery that the earth was not the center of the solar system and the universe led some to question long held beliefs. Many Christians had believed that heaven was a place in the sky directly above the earth. Their belief was that from there God could watch over the earth and its people and angels could descend at times in order to affect the outcome of earthly matters. With the new knowledge, suddenly God and his angels and saints seemed far away.

Perhaps even more surprising to people at that time and later on was Isaac Newton's findings. The common belief that Newton was sitting in his garden when he saw an apple fall to the ground may or not be true. However, he was a brilliant mathematician and, in his calculations, he realized that the moon is tied by gravity to the weightier earth and would also fall to earth except for its high speed rotation around it.

In fact, Newton was the first to describe in mathematical terms how the earth and all the planets are held in their relative positions by the immense gravity of the sun. Though Newton posited gravity as the means by which the planets are kept in orbit around the sun, in his writings he attributed the creation of the solar system to God. He had thought about the matter conscientiously but could see no other way the planets could line up moving in the same direction and in virtually the same plane. Newton didn't know the actual mechanism for how gravity worked. Even today how gravity works remains largely a mystery. However, currently there are some scientists who believe "gravitons" are the means by which gravity works. Yet even to this date this theory remains unproven as gravitons have yet to be observed or measured.

Newton is considered the father of modern science. He demonstrated that nature is describable and predictable following along certain natural laws. He believed that God is responsible for the order in the solar system and in nature. In actuality, Isaac Newton was a Christian who wrote more about religion than about his scientific discoveries. His objective in his religious studies was to arrive at a simple and authentic brand of Christianity which he felt had become corrupted both by Catholicism and to a lesser extent by the

Church of England. He personally did not believe in the Trinity.

Many Enlightenment successors of Newton took a very different view of the universe. They accepted his clocklike view of the workings of the solar system and extrapolated it further. John Locke, whose ideas on government by the consent of those governed led to the American Declaration of Independence, believed that nature always obeys natural laws. Thus, he declared that miracles violate those laws. David Hume, known for his belief that only what we can experience is real for us, argued that with the advancement of scientific knowledge, miraculous explanations for events are unrepeatable and unprovable.

Many leaders of the Enlightenment saw religion in a much different way. They believed in a God who created the universe but not in a God who was personally active in His creation. Their belief was that the universe was made and designed to operate on its own, just as planets continue to go around the sun, without any necessity of a supernatural being to make changes. Because of their belief, they saw God as aloof from His creation including mankind. Deism is the name given to this belief and it was popular among intellectuals of the time and even among some people today. Deists see no need for prayer or even for petition to God in time of need for they do not believe that God has any interest in human beings and their individual concerns.

Notable Americans living in the time of the Enlightenment who held deistic beliefs are Benjamin Franklin and Thomas Jefferson. The latter even went so far as to make his "Jefferson Bible" which records the acts of Jesus and the apostles but with all the miracles and supernatural references removed. The book's actual title is "The Life and Morals of Jesus of Nazareth." Jefferson later wrote of it that the work proved that he was a "real Christian, that is to say, a disciple of the doctrines of Jesus."

Actually, Thomas Jefferson did attend the Anglican or Episcopal church regularly. He is well known as the third president of the United States and for his advocacy of the separation of church and state. He was also a major advocate of literacy, proposing in his home state of Virginia that "all the free children, male and females" should have three years of tax supported primary school education. This was novel at the time as the general population was largely illiterate.

The enlightenment period saw a rise in atheism as well. Some Enlightenment philosophers, particularly Dennis Diderot and Baron D'Holbach were well known atheists in the latter half of the Eighteenth Century. They published their views on atheism and other matters which influenced a number of the people of the time.

A Very Human Saint—Like Us

Many of those recognized as saints didn't start out that way at all. This saint was headstrong, opinionated, courageous and a leader. He even challenged Christ. Then, he did something he regretted.

Many saints were sinners before they changed their lives. St. Augustine is one of the more famous, living with a concubine twelve years before his conversion. St. Paul the evangelist is another, actually persecuting Christians and jailing them before he was thrown from his horse and saw the light. Both of those men wrote volumes and are known largely by what they have written. The saint being considered now wrote little by comparison to them. In fact, the two letters in the New Testament attributed to him are judged by New Testament scholars as being written in his name long after his death. Nevertheless, much has been written about the man. His name? Simon, Petrus, Cephas, Simon Peter, and just Peter.

Peter was like many of us—headstrong, courageous, opinionated, yet a leader, one who jumped to conclusions, one who even tried to tell Jesus he was wrong. Worst of all, he denied even knowing Jesus to save his skin. The story of Peter is that of a real man, a leader, who sometimes got it wrong but, in the end, got it right.

To understand more of him it helps to try to transport ourselves back to life in Israel at the time of Christ. Movies you may have seen usually depict the twelve apostles as middle aged men. That is extremely unlikely. Peter is the only apostle who is known to have had a wife. Marriage at that time in the Holy Land typically came when a young man was about eighteen years of age and a young woman was between thirteen and sixteen. Men were expected and encouraged to marry and, in fact, plans for the event were arranged typically a year before by a couple's parents. The matter of dowery for the bride and groom needed to be settled and written down in a legalistic way.

As for occupations, for the most part occupations were handed down from father to son. Jesus, for example, was a carpenter like his stepfather, Joseph. Peter and his brother Andrew were working at the same calling as their father, John, also a fisherman. We know from the gospels that Zebedee, a fisherman, was the father of the apostles James and John, also fishermen.

Returning to the ages of the apostles, it is significant that, aside from Peter, none of the gospels show that any of Christ's apostles were married. As marriage in Jewish culture at the time was expected and normally mandated by a man and woman's parents, it is significant that none of the twelve apostles were married. For that reason alone, it is most likely that many of the apostles were very young men, men we might call teens today. Other incidents found in the gospels support this belief. In Matthew 20, verses 20-28 the mother of the apostles James and John ask for Jesus to have her sons sit at his right and left sides in his earthly kingdom. Salome's request of Jesus on behalf of her sons seems unlikely if they were mature men. There are many other incidents in scripture that support the surprising youth of the apostles, but now let's get back to Peter.

In John's gospel, Peter's brother Andrew, "having spent a day with Jesus," says to his brother, "We have found the Messiah." Peter may not have left immediately to follow Jesus, for his first words that appear in Luke's gospel are "Go away from me, Lord; I am a sinful man." He and his crew had just caught record numbers of fish after Jesus had told them to let down their nets for a catch. After Peter's words, Jesus said to him, "Don't be afraid; from now on you will catch men." From that point on, Peter and Andrew as well as James and John, who had helped bring in the huge catch of fish, parked their boats and followed Jesus.

Why did these young men so readily leave their profession to follow a man like Jesus? Certainly, there was something about Jesus himself—his voice, his eyes, his demeanor. He had already accomplished the miracle of the huge fish haul when skilled fishermen had worked through the night catching nothing. As noted, there is the likelihood that, with the possible exception of Peter, none of those Christ called were married with families of their own. But why did they so readily follow Jesus? There is a major reason why young men would do so. Israel at that time was a very religious society. Religion was their law in both religious and civil matters with the exception that at the time they were also under the domination of the Roman Empire and her legions. Consequently, to leave one's family occupation to become a Rabbi was the highest calling for a Jewish youth. Parents would be joyful for their sons to be accepted by a Rabbi and to be trained under him.

That Peter was married we know directly because the Gospel of Matthew describes Jesus' healing of his mother-in-law. After her healing, as the gospel states, she waited on Christ and his apostles. This brings up the question of why Peter's own wife didn't wait on the disciples. Why did his mother-in-law have to rise from her sick bed to serve the apostles? Why didn't Peter's wife do it? Had Peter's wife died an early death?

It is true that before modern medicine many women died in childbirth. The Gospels do not say why Peter's wife is absent in the account. Of course, she could have gone to the market or to visit a friend when Jesus and the apostles arrived at their house. There doesn't seem to be any actual facts regarding Peter's wife. Nevertheless, whether true or not, there is a tradition that she went with him to Rome and died there with him during the Roman persecution of Christians in 64 AD.

Of the twelve apostles, Peter, James and John were the three that Jesus seemed to have singled out on different occasions. He took the three of them up a "high mountain" and was transfigured—His face shone like the sun and his clothes became dazzling white. Then Moses and Elijah appeared with Jesus. On seeing this, Peter suggested that three booths or shelters be built there. A bright cloud at that point enveloped them and a voice said, "This is my Son, whom I love; with Him I am well pleased. Listen to Him." The disciples fell to the ground, terrified. "Get up" said Jesus, "Don't be afraid." When they looked up, they saw no-one except Jesus. (Matt 17: 1-6)

Peter may have been more outspoken than some of the other disciples when Jesus asked them, "Who do people say the Son of Man is?" They gave different replies to His question and then Jesus asked the apostles more specifically, "But what about you? Who do you say I am?" It was Simon Peter who answered, "You are Christ, the Son of the living God." It was at this point that Christ told Peter ". . .you are Peter, and on this rock I will build my church. . ." (Matt 16:13-18)

However, it was shortly after this that Peter actually rebuked Jesus. Jesus had just told his apostles that He would suffer at the hands of the elders and chief priests and would be killed and on the third day rise again. Peter took Jesus aside telling him, "Never, Lord! This shall never happen to you!" Jesus turned and said to Peter, "Get behind me, Satan! You are a stumbling block to me; you do not have in mind the things of God, but the things of men." (Matt 16:23)

Peter appears again dramatically in the Garden of Gethsemane. After the Last Supper, Jesus chooses Peter, James and John to go with him to the garden to pray. After they have been there in prayer for some hours, Jesus is apprehended in the darkness when Judas points him out to the soldiers by giving Jesus a kiss. Peter is ready with a sword, likely the only apostle to be thus prepared. In the fracas, Peter cuts off the ear of the high priest's servant. Jesus immediately touches the man's ear, healing him.

Unfortunately, Peter's bravado in the garden soon left him. He and another apostle followed Jesus and the soldiers to where they took Him. The apostle is unnamed in the Gospel account but it likely was John. This apostle knew the servant girl who let them into the courtyard of the high priest. While there, Peter was asked three different times if he was a disciple of Jesus. Each time he answered no, the third time swearing that he didn't even know the man. That's when a cock crowed, just as Jesus had said: "This very night, before the rooster crows, you will disown me three times." (Matt 26:34) On hearing that and remembering Christ's words Peter went out and "wept bitterly."

Following His resurrection, Jesus dramatically forgave Peter by asking him three times "Do you love me?" Peter was grieved at being asked the same question thrice and answered "You know that I love you." In His three responses to each of Peter's answers Jesus tells him to "Feed my lambs," "Take care of my sheep," "Feed my sheep." Jesus is instructing Peter and the other apostles to proclaim the Gospel throughout the world. And that is what Peter and the apostles did, traveling to far countries to spread Christ's message. All of them, except John, died for their faith.

Scientific Discoveries Change the Way We See the World

More recent scientific discoveries seem to show that a Creator was necessary for the creation of the universe and for life, as well as human beings, to be possible. What are the facts behind these discoveries and how do they affect us?

Isaac Newton was a post Renaissance man whose discoveries about gravity and the laws of motion made a huge difference in the thinking of many educated people of his time and after. His finding that the planets are held in place by gravity as they travel around the sun was profound. Before Newton, many people believed that God kept the planets in their correct places in the solar system. After Newton, many people reached the conclusion that it was the impersonal force of gravity that kept the planets in motion.

This finding led many, including Benjamin Franklin and Thomas Jefferson to become Deists. Deists tend to believe that it was God who created the universe but that the creation event was far back in time. They perceived that the planets and the cosmos in general did not need a god to direct the day to day and year to year course of their movements. For that reason, they saw God as an impersonal creator who did not need to attend to the universe or to individuals. They saw God as an aloof god, one who did not take an interest in entering into the lives of people.

People with beliefs like Thomas Jefferson did not believe in personal intercession with God or in miracles. They believed that the laws of nature ruled the universe and that miracles went against those laws and were thus an impossibility. Jefferson famously wrote his own Bible, titled "The Life and Morals of Jesus of Nazareth." Significantly, his bible left out all of Christ's miracles, as well as any reference to the Trinity and Christ's resurrection from the dead.

Others, in Jefferson's time and today, wrote off God completely, becoming atheists and seeing no necessity for God. Still others became agnostics not knowing if there is such a being as God.

The role of a supreme being in the formation of the universe was questioned by scientists as well. In the twentieth century many scientists including the British astronomer Sir Fred Hoyle, astronomer Thomas Gold and

Herman Bondi advanced the idea that the universe had existed from all time in what they termed a "steady state." Albert Einstein originally espoused the steady state theory himself but on further evidence changed his mind. What changed most scientists' thinking was Edwin Hubble's observational discoveries that the universe is expanding, getting larger and larger. That knowledge led him and others to believe that at a time far in the past the universe must have been extremely small, smaller than an atomic particle. Scientists have since determined that at one point in time, now estimated to be 13.7 billion years ago, that tiny extremely hot and dense point erupted in a hot flash to expand and in time create the entire universe with all its galaxies, stars and planets.

For most scientists and for us nonscientists this "Big Bang" event represents the time when the Creator caused everything to come into existence. Many Christians are also of the belief that the Big Bang was God's plan for starting the universe.

Another major discovery from the twentieth century was the remarkable detection of the properties of DNA. DNA is short for deoxyribonucleic acid which is an essential component of all living things whether they be human, animal, insect or plant. Discovered initially by Rosalind Franklin some years earlier, James Watson and Francis Crick, building on Franklin's findings, in 1957 elucidated the structure of DNA molecules.

What is the importance of DNA to us today? A simple answer is that it is through our DNA, imparted half by our mother and half by our father that we are genetically encoded to share the genes of our parents. If they are tall, we will likely be tall, if white or black we will be the same, and to an extent we are likely to have similar facial features as our father or mother. It is the same with animals and other creatures. A monkey's offspring will always be monkeys, a carrot seed will always become a carrot and the egg of a bird will always become a bird.

What is perplexing to many, scientists included, is how this could have happened. DNA is an amazingly complex molecule. Bill Gates famously said, "DNA is like a computer program but far, far more advanced than any software ever created." That this necessary stuff of life could have arisen on its own at the beginning of life on earth through natural processes defies imagination. No scientist has been able to show how this could have happened though some have had theories. For most Christians, as well as many of those of other faiths, the beginning of life on earth came about through the hand of God.

If, like most scientists today, we accept that the universe began approximately 13.7 years ago in a Big Bang, how did it happen that from the initial tiny kernel all the galaxies, stars and planets arose? A simple answer is God did it. For the majority of people that may explain it sufficiently. Astrophysicists who study the matter know that the universe that we are a part of could only have happened under certain very precise conditions or laws. What is almost mind boggling and yet true is that without these very precise laws the entire universe as well as mankind would not exist. For those with an interest in science I'll list some of the major ones here briefly.

The first is gravity. We encounter the effects of gravity when we are only babies. At first, we crawl and then in time we make our first attempts to walk. We have to be careful because if we make a misstep gravity pulls us down to the floor. Gradually, we learn how to work with the ever present gravity though we feel its effects when we lift a bag of cement or a heavy bag of potatoes. Thanks to Issac Newton and other scientists we know that gravity is the force that keeps the earth and planets moving around the sun and our own moon circling the earth. Actually, gravity is extremely important in keeping the whole universe in order.

The second major force that has a tremendous influence on our lives is electromagnetism. The application of this force of nature only began to be understood in the nineteenth century. By the end of the century, thanks to Thomas Edison and his invention of a long lasting electric light bulb, wealthy people could have generators installed in their homes to provide electricity. By 1920, large power stations and electric wiring brought electricity to the homes of those living in towns and then later to those living in the country. Finally, after many thousands of years of human history, light bulbs replaced candles and oil lamps. Today, some people buy their own generators to provide electric power in case of power outages. The usefulness of the electromagnetic force is all encompassing. It powers our lamps, radios, TV's, computers, toasters, cell phones, garage door openers and so much more. In another simple way, the magnetic force also has the very practical use of holding our notes and other objects to our refrigerators.

A third major force of nature is named "the strong force" or the "strong nuclear force." It exists within us and in fact in all matter. Without the strong force acting within each atom of our bodies, and indeed in all matter, there would be nothing of a physical nature at all. There could be no tables, chairs, trees, or even planets or stars. The strong force keeps atoms together by binding the electrons and protons such that they don't fly off into space. It is also the force within stars and our own sun that creates the powerful energy that creates sunlight to make plants grow. The force is also used in major nuclear power plants across the world to generate electricity.

The immense power of the strong forces is also utilized in the atomic bomb and the hydrogen bomb. The latter is estimated to be one thousand times more powerful than the atomic bomb that was dropped on Hiroshima. The United States tested such a bomb on an uninhabited Bikini atoll in 1954. It turned out to be much more powerful than anticipated. In fact, it was so powerful that nuclear radiation settled onto islands 100 and 300 miles away causing sickness and loss of hair and even death. The US government needed to pay many millions of dollars of reparations to the families of those who died or were injured by the fallout.

What is called "the weak force" is another critical fundamental force. Of all the four major forces of nature it is the hardest to understand or explain. Merriam Webster defines it as "a fundamental physical force that governs interactions between hadrons and leptons (as in the emission and absorption of neutrinos) and is responsible for particle decay processes (such as beta decay) in radioactivity, that is 10^{-5} times the strength of the strong force, and that acts over distances smaller than those between nucleons in an atomic nucleus." (If you understand that, you are a true scientist.) The force has been quantified and its overriding importance for mankind is that in its essential nature it provides the catalyst for nuclear fusion in stars and our sun. Without the weak force the sun would not shine nearly bright enough to provide photosynthesis for plants and to warm the earth.

Where did these laws come from? No human being had anything to do with them. As well as scientists can determine, they have existed at least since the beginning of the universe. That takes us back to the Big Bang. Scientists know that without these laws of nature a big bang might still have been a possibility but the entire universe and later our solar system and earth could not have come into existence. It is evident that these laws were programmed into the universe since the beginning of time. Astrophysicists know that these four individual laws must have been precisely set at the values they have or there would be no life on earth. To me, it is the work of God.

The Reality of Our World

As we know from Einstein's most famous equation $E = MC^2$, energy and matter can be transposed. What has been determined is that a single gram of matter transposed into energy will create 21 kilotons of energy, similar to the blast that leveled the city of Nagasaki. Before modern science and recent times people thought that the world and everything in it is composed of mostly solid matter. However, we now know that the atoms that make up everything, our bodies, our houses, our furniture and automobiles are basically empty.

Yes, any scientific article on the nature of atoms will reveal that atoms are more than 99.9999% empty space. That means that everything we touch and observe is far less than one percent solid. Yet it is true that we feel solidity in our walls, our chairs and in everything we touch. Why? The explanation given is that the atoms of each object, our bodies, our chairs, walls, etc. repel those in any other object. That is why we feel it when we hit something and feel pain when anything pierces our body, even if it is only a pin prick or paper cut.

Nevertheless, our actual physicality is minimal such that if the empty spaces within all the atoms in our body were taken away each of us would be far smaller than a grain of salt. As such, it seems we are far more spiritual than physical beings. It is mainly the electrons in each atom of our body moving at roughly five million miles an hour that sustains us in a living state.

That's enough science. Next, let's take a look at some human concerns that affect each of us.

Life, One Day at a Time

Our childhood experiences can directly affect our outlook on life. Nevertheless, we as human beings are immensely talented. Despite everything, we know that life has its ups and downs. How we deal with them is important to us and to our families.

We personally have nothing to do with it. We are conceived, live in our mother's womb, and usually about nine months later enter the world. It is obvious that at birth we have very little knowledge although we have the instinct to suck and we like the feel of our skin against the warmth of the skin of our mother. Our vision is blurry at birth but our hearing is good and we likely recognize the voice of our mother and our father from hearing them talking while inside the womb.

We are positively full of potential at that time of our life and we soak up everything that happens to us and around us. Babyhood is an important time of life and we quickly learn what kind of world we have been born into. Are our cries for milk and attention answered soon enough so we learn that we have the power with our voice to get what we need? Or, are we left alone such that our cries go unanswered for long periods of time? If the former, we feel we have some control of our needs. If the latter, we may feel powerless to get the sustenance we need.

Yes, early on we learn that we have some power or else we learn we have very little ability to have some control over our environment. The pattern continues as we grow into toddlers. Are we able to actively take our part in the lives of those most important to us.? Do they cuddle us, talk to us, listen to our first attempts to talk.? Do they excitedly smile back when we manage our first smile? Do they love to hold us, to talk to us and to include us in their activities? Or, are they too busy to provide anything other than the most basic care so that we have enough food to live?

Of course, our parent(s) may have other reasons for not caring for us. They may have significant health issues, may be depressed, may have sudden family loss of income or be encountering other major concerns that distract them from caring for a young child. As children, we have no way of knowing, but we definitely can feel neglected if they park us for long hours in out of the way places or in front of their TV which we do not comprehend. Unfortunately, how we are treated in our early life can affect our early conception of ourselves as young people who are either loved and cared for or not.

This continues as we grow and mature into the primary grades and then into our teens. We know by then if we are really loved and cherished or if we are only given enough to survive and otherwise feel ignored or are told in so many ways that we are unimportant or even a burden. Yes, in our early years we develop a conception of ourselves that often remains with us the rest of our lives. Will it be one of self confidence and an outgoing spirit or one of reserve and questioning if our lives are really worthwhile? It is easy to make friends when you're outgoing, but difficult when you're reserved and have a low opinion of yourself. Unfortunately, the teen years are the time when things can become so difficult in one's mind that even the contemplation of suicide is possible. Also, unfortunately, social media can exacerbate the problem.

Obviously, the gift of being born into a loving family is important although it is nothing we can control. My mother, God rest her soul, was probably not the best at raising her three children. However, she likely didn't have the best example because her own mother died in a fire when she was only a toddler. As we, her children, were growing up, mom usually tended to look on the negative side of things. In fact, as I recall, one of her favorite songs was "Mama said there'll be days like this." Unfortunately, she went into a deep depression when my father died after three heart attacks at the age of fifty nine. My uncle in California tried to help her for about a year with doctors, psychiatrists and various treatments but when she came back to Indiana it was up to me and my two sisters to arrange care for her.

Mom's depression was so devastating that none of us could actually live with her without getting depressed ourselves. We found apartments for her close enough that she could walk to a store (she didn't drive). We would invite her to dinners at our house or out to restaurants and helped her to live on the little social security she got from my father's employment. I believe the reason for her continuing deep depression was that she simply wouldn't take her medication. It was not until many years later when my younger sister was able to get her into a nursing home where they insisted on her taking her pills that mom became a levelheaded and an actually loving mother.

As human beings we know that life has its ups and downs. Perfect happiness is not to be achieved on earth although for short periods of time we may come close to experiencing it. None of us is perfect. We make mistakes and those we love and depend on make mistakes too. Greed enters our life and the desire to be number one, or at least to be recognized, seems to be a constant challenge for us.

I think at least part of the reason for this is because we as human beings are so talented. Some excel in music, others in business, others in sports, others on stage and a few of us are quite handsome or beautiful. It's easy to let these God given gifts go to our heads. For those with particular talents it can be easy to seek the acclaim of others and not cultivate our relationships with our spouse, our family, and even our children. It is so sad but it very often happens that a couple that begins with so much love ends up not being able to stand each other.

Some Downsides of Modern Times

We do not live in a "golden age" regardless of our scientific advancements. Concerns arise that are endemic to the times we find ourselves in. How we deal with them can have much to do with our level of happiness.

It can be said that every age has its ups and downs. Our times are no different. There are a great many good aspects of our living today in the twenty first century. These will be discussed in the next chapter. Now, we will discuss some negatives of living in the current age. Why focus on them? Because if we are aware of them, we can take steps to deal with them.

Where to start? It is true that the world we live in today is very different from that of one hundred years ago or even fifty years ago. It is definitely not the same world our grandparents lived in. We might note that older houses made room for only one car, not for two or three. My parents were atypical, we didn't have a car at all until I was thirteen years old. We walked everywhere or took the bus. I think that in general people walked much more than they do today just in the course of getting from one place to another. Unless people take time for sports or to work out in a gym or facility, people tend to get less exercise. Jobs in factories and in warehouses have largely become mechanized. I think back to the two garbage men who in our neighborhood unloaded the cans into the back of the vehicle. Today the driver directs a mechanical arm to lift the trash barrels and place them into truck.

Children don't play outside in unsupervised sports and activities as much as was common years ago. My own two sons would quite often in the summer disappear after lunch and only return at suppertime. They were out with friends playing games or just enjoying nature. Today, unsupervised sports and activities is much less common. Children seem happy to sit in their homes with their phones or other devices playing games or connecting with others online. Thankfully, many parents are active in getting their children into sports and activities where they can get some exercise and develop friendships.

However, for parents themselves as well as those who are single, getting exercise, even if only taking walks, is often forgotten. Many people have to work long hours at stressful jobs and even at home may be called to deal with situations arising from their employment. Lack of exercise is one reason why obesity rates have been climbing in America for many years. The CDC shows that in sixty years, from the early 1960's to modern times, the obesity rate has more than tripled from about 13% to over 41% of Americans. The rate for children has also more than tripled from the seventies to today from 5% to 19%. Is it because of the time children spend on their screen rather than enjoying outdoor activities? Or, is it because children's TV shows have for many years been advertising sugary cereals and snacks.

There's another reason why Americans are getting heavier. Many more individuals and families are eating out far more than they used to and, if not eating out, bringing in food from restaurants. A newer trend becoming popular is to buy already prepared foods directly from supermarkets and other stores. Typically, dining out and even brought in meals tend to be saltier and larger in size than home cooked meals. Furthermore, if the studies are correct, Americans are simply eating more than they used to even though they are on average less physically active than in times past.

All this of course has health implications. The increasing numbers of people with diabetes is one, and the growing number of those who need to have knee and hip replacement surgery is likely another. Fortunately, modern medicine is allowing many of us to live longer even with health complications.

Another problem that has arisen in modern times is theft. In times past not everyone bothered to lock their doors and their cars at night. Most of us feel the need to do so today. Pickpockets have always been around, particularly in popular, touristy places. Today, now that we are very often using credit cards and other means of electronic payment, thieves have found ways to make purchases on our credit cards. Years ago, we used a card to make a medical payment and the clerk was subsequently able to copy the card number to make many hundreds of dollars of purchases of her own.

Today, we have to be alert and careful that all our online accounts are protected with passwords known only to us. We also have to be very careful what we click on because a site may contain a computer virus or worse. I did that once and had to pay a significant amount of money to have the virus removed so I could continue to use my computer. Sometimes thieves are right out in the open. Once, years ago while taking a walk during my lunch hour in downtown Hammond, Indiana, I was approached by a man who acted very suspiciously toward me. Standing at my side, something he said alarmed me. Might it have been a hold up? I don't know for sure, but for the only time in my life I swiftly ran away from the man.

Mental Health

Most of this chapter has to do with some of the downsides of living in the modern age. Not that this is a bad age to live in but any age has problems of its own, including the Biblical times when Christ walked the earth, as well as past times in our own history. The next chapter will change focus to look at all the good aspects of living in the present age.

As for mental health one might question whether it is only a topic focused on today that has always been with us, or if mental health problems are actually increasing. In recent years there has been a major focus on mass murders. Not surprising, as they have been increasing in frequency in recent times. As they are sometimes directed at innocent children, the grief and the fear have increased dramatically. Some children have internalized the terror to such an extent that they are actually afraid to go to school. I sincerely wish our country would take measures to make these shootings rare if not nonexistent. Certainly, while school shootings have happened in other countries, they have been absent or extremely rare by comparison to those in the United States.

As much as mass murders and school shootings are a huge concern in the United States, what comes next may come as a surprise. Homicides are down. Following the end of the

Covid pandemic, the rate of murders in our country has shown a dramatic decline according to FBI records. Homicide has dropped in most of the large cities of the country. Specifics are, New York 12% decrease according the NYPD, Los Angeles homicide rate down over 15% based on the Los Angeles Police Department, Chicago down 13% according to Chicago police data, Houston down 22% according to police data, Phoenix down 14% according to the Phoenix Police department and in Philadelphia, the sixth largest city, the homicide rate is down more than 20% according to the Philadelphia Police department. Was the higher homicide rate during the covid epidemic caused by covid restrictions?

What may be more interesting is that looking at FBI crime reporting over time, the 1990's featured far higher rates of homicides then in recent years. The rate during those years reached 9 murders per 100,000 people. That high 1990's rate, as more recent statistical information shows, has currently declined to a little over 5 murders per 100,000 people.

Hopefully, the homicide rates for modern times will continue to decrease now that Covid restrictions and closures are over. However, another alarming national trend has arisen. While homicides have been trending down, suicides rates are trending up and have actually been increasing since the pandemic. In contrast to current record keeping showing a little over 5 homicides per 100,000 people, recent reporting is currently showing 14 suicides per 100,000 people in 2023 alone. Clearly, people are ending their lives at a much higher rate than violent offenders are taking them.

The most recent statistics available show that while almost 20,000 people in America died by homicide, over 50,000 died by suicide. There is one thing they have in common: both homicides and successful suicides are in most cases perpetrated with firearms. Suicide by other means, for example cutting and poisoning, are often unsuccessful and usually give a person time to think if they really want to go through with taking their lives. Suicide with a gun is quick, cannot be reversed and is usually fatal. Who commits suicide? Males, both young and old, are far more likely than women to commit suicide. In fact, in the United States they do so at a more than four to one rate over females.

The United States Center for Disease Control, the CDC, keeps records on causes of death in America. The startling statistic is that after accidental death, suicide is the leading cause of death in the US of those aged 10 to 14. For the next age group, 15-24 it is the third leading cause of death closely following homicide. In the 25-34 age group, suicide again comes in as the second leading cause of death. For those 35 and older suicide is still a death factor but other causes including heart disease, cancer, covid 19 and diabetes mellitus are more likely to be the reason for death. These statistics may be somewhat old now but they are compiled from of a long range study done between 2001 and 2021. It seems unlikely that going forward we are likely to see major changes.

As mentioned, many suicide attempts do not result in death, but suicide by a firearm is usually fatal. Guns are readily available in America. The latest statistics show that there are 120 guns registered in the US for every 100 people. This is far more than any other country. Only the Falkland Islands with 62 per 100 and Yemen with 53 per 100 people come close. Other countries, including a few that some of us have visited, include Switzerland, 28 per 100 people, Germany and France 20 per 100, Italy, 14 per 100, Russia 12 per 100 and Great Britain, 5 people owning guns for every 100 citizens.

Unlike the great majority of countries, the right to gun ownership is written into law with the second amendment protecting the right of every mature citizen to keep and bear arms. At the time of our country's founding, the land of United States was a relative wilderness compared to the high population densities in most of Europe. People needed firearms for hunting and in some parts of the country to protect against the possibility of uprisings of native American Indians.

There were no repeating weapons when the law was established. The weapon most commonly in use at the time the Constitution was written was the Long Land Pattern Musket. Both sides in the American revolutionary war against the British used the musket, or the "Brown Bess" as it was commonly called. This smoothbore muzzleloader weighed about ten pounds and required a number of steps to load. It was a complicated process. A paper cartridge held the musket ball and the powder and a soldier needed to open a paper cartridge, normally with his teeth, pour a little of it into the flash pan and then pour the rest of the powder down the barrel followed by the musket ball. Then he would push the paper down with the ramrod, thus sealing the ball in the barrel making the gun ready for shooting. As complex as this may sound, soldiers went through many weeks of training and after completion were expected to be able to load and fire three times in a minute. They didn't have much time to actually aim the rifle, only to point it across the way toward the enemy soldiers on the other side.

One final but important note on suicides before leaving this depressing and distressing topic. Suicides among teens and young adults have seen increases that have been linked to extensive use of social media. Prior to the year 2000 many people and most teens did not have access to cell phones. Now, they are in the hands of everyone including most preteens in the United States. Phones are really miniature computers that bring the news of the world as well as the activities of our friends into our hands. Youths who may have had a falling out with friends very often know from their social media when they are being excluded from social events. The sense of isolation that can result for young people who are "different" in any way can be devastating for some.

Of course, we are all different, some of us are more social than others, although each of us normally has our own interests and passions. Physically, we are all very different as well. When I look around in any place where there is a gathering of people, the variety of body types is simply amazing to me. There are heavy people, those who are quite tall and some quite short as well as those who are robust and those who are frail looking. Our former next door neighbor was extremely slender, with a figure like a preteen; her older daughter was our first babysitter. Then there are guys whose torso is so massive that they have almost no neck.

For those of us who are older, we can usually appreciate our differences, but for young people, particularly those with little love or encouragement at home, being different can be tough. Young people have so much potential and can ultimately do so much if they begin to recognize their individual talents and abilities. Those of us who are their parents, relatives, friends and associates need to be encouraging, to cut them some slack and help them to realize their potential.

A Wonderful Country—America

American knowhow and ingenuity have contributed greatly to our health and comfort. We have a spacious, beautiful land where people can even choose what type of climate they prefer. In health, major American contributions have enabled us to live longer, healthy lives.

The United States is a great country; we have much to be thankful for. A spacious land, we have areas in the far south where it seldom gets cold and places in the far north where there are not many days of warm temperatures. Our great land is linked together by major highways, thanks to major construction begun in the Eisenhower administration and continued by other presidents, such that we can travel great distances, much of it on free expressways.

Because of its extensive size, Americans need never worry about droughts or late frosts in one part of the country greatly affecting our food supply. Yes, prices go up when some things are in short supply, but we are always likely to have plenty to eat. If we have bad weather in one area of the country, we can get our agricultural products from another state.

Similarly, people can often choose where they want to live. If they want warmth they can choose to live in states like Florida and Arizona. Retired people with money often live in warm states in the winter and return to colder states during months when the weather is warmer. Few countries can offer these advantages to their citizens.

One of the historically newer countries of the world, the United States also has one of the least dense populations. When people from Europe first arrived, they found a largely empty land filled with indigenous Indian tribes who for the most part did not build permanent towns or cities. The Indian tribes were never populous and having only hatchets, knives and bows and arrows were usually defeated in battles when faced with gunfire. However, what really devastated Indian peoples was the diseases Europeans brought with them to the new land. Indians had never encountered these afflictions and it has been estimated that up to 90% of the native population died of diseases like smallpox, measles and flu.

The only American Indian proclaimed a saint, Saint Kateri Tekakwitha, is a prime example of this. Both her parents died in a smallpox epidemic and she herself had permanent scars on her face and suffered partial blindness as a result of the disease. Saint Kateri was noted for her works of charity among her people and came to be known as the "Lily of the Mohawks" for her kindness, faith, prayer and heroic suffering. She died shortly before her 24th birthday of tuberculosis. Her last words were, "Jesos Konoronkwa" ("Jesus, I love you.") Those near her said that the scars on her face disappeared at her death.

Today, after many generations of growth, including major immigrations of Europeans, Asians and those from Mexico and South America, the United States still retains a rather low population density. Recent worldwide statistics on the number of people shows America has an average of 91 people per square mile. Certainly, within cities like New York, Boston and Chicago density is far higher. However, in the country as a whole, 91 people compares to other countries with far greater population densities. For examples, Germany, has 600 people per square mile, Italy, 510, France, 300, the United Kingdom, 720, Spain, 240, Ireland, 190, Poland, 310 and Japan, 840. There are a few countries with lesser population densities than the US, including Russia with 21 people per square mile, Canada, 10 and Australia 9. As these numbers show, America still has much room for growth.

American is blessed not only with space but also with talent. Many of the things we now take for granted were pioneered by American prowess and ingenuity. The first that comes to mind is the automobile, developed by Henry Ford. The Model T came out in 1908 and Ford's production line system made the car affordable for millions of Americans. It actually sold for $825 in the first year and became even cheaper in subsequent years.

Another is the radio, developed by an Italian, Guglielmo Marconi. However, Marconi's radio could only transmit dots and dashes, which is wireless telegraphy. Reginald Fessenden, a Canadian working in the United States, made substantial improvements to radio transmission. He succeeded for the first time, in the year 1900, in sending the human voice across the airwaves.

Another major invention was the incandescent light bulb developed by Thomas Edison. Edison was not the first person to make a light bulb but he was the first to develop an affordable bulb, in 1880, that would last for 1200 hours. After the development of incandescent lighting, it took time to set up generating stations and to run wires to individual homes and factories. By 1919 only 6% of American homes had electricity. Twenty years later, two thirds of American homes had incandescent lighting. Can you imagine having to light candles or oil lamps to be able to see anything at night? It's no wonder that before electrical lighting the majority of people for much of the year went to bed at nightfall and got up at the rising of the sun. The song "The Old Lamplighter" recalls those days when towns actually employed people to go around and light streetlights in some of the more populous cities.

An American also played a major role in the development of television. Scientists from many different countries had been working on the concept, but it was Philo Farnsworth, an American from Utah, who made critical contributions to electronic television that makes possible fully functional video today. His Farnsworth Television and Radio Corporation operated in Fort Wayne, Indiana from 1938 to 1951.

Television was a real game changer. It first became available in 1939. By 1950 20% of Americans had a TV and by 1960 nearly 90% owned one. Radio soon lost many listeners and movie theaters saw a major drop off in attendance. Today people often watch their favorite channels for many hours each day. Some don't like to turn off their television at all, preferring to hear the background sound instead of a quiet house.

Today, the biggest electronic medium in many of our lives is the internet. It is readily available now that just about everyone older than ten or so has their own personal cellphone. No more having to find a phone to call someone in an emergency or any situation. The calling boxes that were present on miles of Florida highways and those of other states have long since been removed, for today almost no one travels without their phone. What is amazing to me is that less than 100 years ago hardly anyone had even a "landline" phone with the ability to call anyone let alone a handy cellphone. Communication with family and friends back then depended on letters, or if something was really urgent, one could send a short message via a Western Union telegraph office.

As much as our lives have been changed by electronic technology, a real revolution has also occurred in health care, much to our benefit. It may be hard to believe that in 1935, when social security was enacted during the Roosevelt administration, the typical lifespan for men was 61 years of age and for women it was 65. Eligibility for social security assistance was set at 65 years of age and later was reduced to age 62 for reduced social security benefits. Today, one can retire at 62 and receive benefits although waiting until full retirement age, presently set at age 67, results on average a 50% higher social security check.

Why are people living longer? Medical breakthroughs are the reason. For most of recorded history large families were the norm. However, it was extremely common for one or more children to die at an early age from "childhood" diseases. Today, thanks to the work of Americans and scientists of other countries, most of those diseases have been brought under control. Dr. Maurice Hilleman, PhD from the University of Chicago, alone is responsible for eight vaccines—

among them measles, mumps, hepatitis A and B, chickenpox, streptococcus, and influenza. Smallpox, probably the worst killer of children and adults, began to be controlled in the years after 1796 when Dr. Edward Jenner of England successfully tested his smallpox inoculations.

Thanks to Dr. Jonas Salk, the son of Jewish immigrants living in New York City, polio was effectively eradicated. It had taken the lives or incapacitated millions in the United States and other countries in the first half of the twentieth century. By the end of the 1970's the disease was practically eliminated in the United States, though to this day it remains a danger in certain parts of the world.

Dr. Salk's work was supported by President Franklin D. Roosevelt, himself a polio survivor, who was paralyzed from the waist down. Today, children routinely receive vaccinations before attending school. All the states and territories of the United States currently have vaccination requirements for children attending both school and childcare centers.

Health care has seen dramatic improvement in other ways, not only with vaccinations giving people much better chances of avoiding infectious diseases. Important developments in the last ten, twenty and fifty years have had major health benefits for everyone, seniors in particular. Sixty or so years ago there was little doctors could do to repair blocked arteries in people with heart disease. Heart disease, and with it heart attacks, to this day remains the number one cause of death in the United States. In my family it seems endemic, my grandfather and father died of it, and I and my slender sister, a vegetarian, both suffered heart attacks.

While doctors could do little for my grandfather and not too much for my father, for my sister and I a stent threaded through an artery was what was needed to solve the problem. No longer do doctors usually need to do open heart surgery as they had to do some years ago to ameliorate blocked arteries in the heart. Thankfully, my sister and I, and one of my tennis friends can remain as physically active as before without much concern.

The second leading cause of death in the United States is cancer. Unfortunately, statistics show that cancer is increasing. However, the good news is that deaths from cancer are decreasing. But why is cancer increasing? Those who did a study published in BMJ Oncology cite poor diets, as well as alcohol and tobacco use. Inactive life styles and obesity may very well be one cause of increasing cancer rates. There is also a genetic proclivity among some families to develop certain kinds of cancer. Certainly, the average adult American is far heavier than forty or fifty years ago, likely a contributing factor. While there is as yet no cure on the horizon for cancer, research is continuing with the hope that a breakthrough will be found.

In other areas, medical science has made tremendous strides. No longer need tens of millions of Americans rely on canes or crutches to get along with bad shoulders, knees or hips. Surgery for these conditions has considerably improved and it is not at all unusual for one to have hip surgery one month and return to playing tennis, golf, bowling or pickle ball a few months later.

The need for these kinds of surgeries may partially be the result of the general average increase in weight of Americans, but not always. A doctor I know liked to run marathons in cities of both the United States and Europe. The pounding his knees took running on pavement likely led him to later need to have double knee replacement. However, today, many years later, he remains an avid golfer, choosing to walk the eighteen hole golf course several times a week both in summer and winter.

Replacement surgery is still a major operation and requires that one set aside significant time and commitment for physical therapy in order to get back strength and agility. It is therefore not a cure all, particularly for the very elderly or otherwise compromised individuals.

Last to be discussed here is the modern miracle of cataract surgery. Most of us, by the time we reach 40 or 50 realize we can't focus as closely as before to be able to clearly see fine print. The need to hold things farther away to see becomes necessary. The loss of sharp close range eyesight is normal with age and is easily fixed by cheap reading glasses found at most retailers. Later in life, usually between the ages of 60 and 80, the vast majority of people will develop cataracts, which obscure normal vision making things harder to see and a bit darker than with good eyesight.

Fortunately, thanks to another American doctor and scientist, Dr. Charles Kelman, what used to a somewhat dangerous eye operation to correct the problem has since become rather routine. In cataract surgery today, much thanks to Dr. Kelman, instead of ten days of hospitalization, the procedure is done in a specialized office setting and the patient is sent home the same day. Having had cataract surgery on one eye myself, I can say it was like a miracle. What was my bad eye before the relatively minor operation has become my good eye! Nevertheless, not everyone is completely happy with the results. Consequently, I think it is important to consult with an ophthalmologist before cataract surgery to be informed, especially as there are a number of different options available.

Why Religion may be More Difficult Today

There are many reasons why church attendance and religious belief seems to be in decline in some parts of the world, particularly in the United States and much of Europe. This section discusses those reasons and offers some suggestions on how we can personally deal with the situation.

Older people may remember when it seemed like almost everyone went to church—every Sunday. Today, that is not the case at all. Many don't go and others attend on an irregular basis. What could be the reason for this decline? There are many reasons given and those who are church leaders have been investigating them. Some churches have made significant changes to draw more people to services.

It is commonly thought that we live in a secular age. There is much truth in the belief. Aside from that, there are those who point out many flaws in churchmen and women. According to a long term study done by the John Jay College of Criminal Justice, "4,392 priests and deacons had allegations of child sexual abuse during the years of 1950 to 2002 against 10,667 children." That the Church tried to cover up many of these cases made it all the more reprehensible. The data indicates that approximately 4% of all the priests in the United States were found to have made improper advances toward youths during the 52 year time period. This comes to approximately one out of 25 priests.

To put this in some context, research from the U.S. Department of Education found that about 5 to 7 percent of public school teachers engaged in similar sexually abusive behavior with their students during a similar time frame. Approximately 50 years is a large time span and during that time period incidents of abuse were more prevalent in the earlier years, particularly in the nineteen-seventies. Adjustments and closer monitoring is being done, both in religious and academic arenas, to significantly reduce these kinds of incidents.

These cases of sexually abusive behavior in most denominations have likely had the effect of turning some away from religious services. In recent years it is probable that far more people have left for other reasons. Some departed during

Covid and decided not to return. Others, particularly young people, leave when they're away at college for most of the year. Long hours and weekend work schedules can make regular attendance difficult for others. For some parents, when children have games and even practices scheduled on Sundays, church attendance can become more difficult. Other situations, include moving away and not connecting with a new church, and leaving when a particular minister or pastor retires or moves to another church, are reasons that are frequently given.

One major reason that is usually not mentioned by those no longer attending services is the tremendous rise in social media and its effects. People in general spend far more time interacting with social media than they do inside a church. In fact, the rise of this medium has become quite pervasive in the past twenty or so years. Since at least the turn of the century, most adults, teens and even many children use cell phones on a regular basis, if not somewhat constantly. It goes without saying that for most of us the main use of our phones is not to make phone calls. Just as with our laptops and our other devices, our little hand held computers bring us the world along with important contacts with friends and relatives.

With the rise in our use of the internet, the number of commercials each of us see daily has likely more than quadrupled. Even as I'm typing this book, advertisements sometimes appear. When I check my email all kinds of ads pop up.

When I watch TV, ads take up much of the programming time. Even when I watch sport events the play-by-play announcers make additional pitches for one thing or another. I'm sure it's what they're required to do. This is a major change, especially with regard to our phones and computers, and it cannot fail to affect each of us more than we realize.

Our usual response to the ads is to mentally turn them off—we don't want or need to know about most of the things they are offering. However, ads are meticulously crafted to tap into our desires, fears, and aspirations. Untold billions of dollars are spent to design them, some using celebrities to draw our attention, and to air them where we can't miss seeing and hearing them.

How do we typically react to advertising? For the most part, I think we turn away or try to pay no attention to almost all the ads except the few that spark our interest. As a result, we become conditioned to react negatively to much of the content we see. We can, and I believe many of us do, extrapolate that type of conditioning to our own lives and even to the Church. Advertising can make us see our own lives as not as well off, not as glamorous or not as successful as those seen on our screens. Studies confirm that exposure to more advertising correlates to a lower individual self image. This may be particularly true for youth, girls in particular, who through viewing women and girls with apparently perfect lives, flawless and often photoshopped faces and bodies, can easily see themselves as dull and unattractive.

As for church, our experience in reacting negatively to the great bulk of the advertising we encounter can and may very often extend to how we feel about our church. Because we have to be critical not to be taken in by the lure of advertisers trying to have us buy their products, we can easily develop a critical frame of mind that becomes natural for us even when attending religious services. Maybe we didn't like a particular sermon or didn't like the emphasis on monetary collections or even Pastor Jim's apparent favoritism toward certain parishioners. When we think about it, there may be other things we don't really like. Basically, we can become negative even within our own church.

Rather than joining in what is bound to be an imperfect community of believers, some of us may turn away because it is not perfect. However, it is realistic to understand that people will always be imperfect, even good Christian people. That includes pastors, deacons, nuns, elders of the church and ourselves.

We cannot escape our imperfect world. We know that we ourselves are far from perfect, as is our family, our spouses and our children. But we love them and they (hopefully) love us in return. We participate in a much less than perfect world whether it is where we work, where we recreate and at our clubs and organizations including our church. It's the world that Christ came to make better and to save. As He said, "I have not come to call the righteous but sinners to repentance." (Luke 5:32)

The Religious Advantage

According to surveys and some testing, atheists tend to be smarter than average. That doesn't mean they are happier. It also doesn't mean they will live longer. There are definite plusses to religious faith. This section discusses these issues and offers insight into how we can be open to finding peace and, if desired, God in our lives.

Not everyone wants or cares for religion. Studies indicate that in modern times more people are choosing atheism or agnosticism. Choosing the latter is likely a consequence of simply not knowing if there is a God or not. Many people today grow up in homes where religion and belief are simply not part of their upbringing. Others learn in school about natural science, evolution and cosmology and find little or no mention of the concept of God.

If the studies are accurate that atheists are smarter than average, it may make sense that they don't necessarily go along with the religious majority. They are comfortable in going their own separate way. They may also be more likely to think things out for themselves and come to their own conclusions. However, on the whole they may do so at their own disadvantage.

A number of studies show that atheists and agnostics live shorter lives by several years than their religious brethren. Another study indicates that on average atheists are more likely than others to smoke and drink which in itself could be a contributing factor to a shorter lifespan. This may be especially true of smoking with its medically known effects on health. Other studies show that atheists are not as happy as those who attend Church services on a regular basis. The evidence is that being part of a religious community is important socially, and when tough times come church members can be solicitous as well as provide assistance.

Nevertheless, despite these findings, it is unlikely that a true atheist will decide to become a church member. Atheists have learned to trust in their beliefs, or in this case their unbelief. I personally think that most atheists are not "against God," only that their lack of belief is because they don't see God.

In contrast, a religious person, especially one strong in their faith, sees God in nature, in their family and friends and in their own heart. We might well inquire how two different people can see things so differently. Frankly, I can't speak from the atheist's point of view. I am sure there are many who can do so, some quite eloquently. Likewise, there are Christians past and present who can address their belief in God eloquently. Personally, I can only say how I see things.

I wasn't always a "good boy." Before the age of sixteen I had tried smoking and drinking. Had marijuana been around at my early age I'm sure I would have tried that as well. I also had a temper and got into a number of fights, including a fistfight with my best friend. So, I was going nowhere in high school, and getting poor grades despite being tested for fairly high intelligence. Then, at a school retreat the priest presenter did something that no school would allow today. He fired a gun into the air in the midst of his talk and said "Jesus died for you!" Naturally that caught everyone's attention, mine in particular.

That revelation turned me around. I reformed my young life, started going to church sometimes even on weekdays and went from being a C student to making a regular appearance at each grading period on the honor roll, sometimes the high honor roll. What was the difference? I think it was that I suddenly came to the realization that Jesus actually cared about me. Like many, I didn't have the most loving parents, God rest their souls. So, I think that knowing that someone loved me, God himself, added motivation and purpose to my life. Of course, as any of us who have lived for more than a few years know, life will always have its up and downs. Belief in God doesn't equate to a carefree life.

Much later, during the time we were engaged to be married, the girl I was engaged to told me she was breaking our relationship. I definitely didn't see this coming. Unfortunately, the week before I had been notified that I was no longer needed at my job. Was that the reason she left? I was so distraught that I sought out counseling. I needed to know if I was sane. After scheduling a meeting with a psychologist and talking to him for a time, he ended up telling me that I was OK, only upset at the circumstances. Good news, but it didn't change how I felt. Fortunately, two months later a job I had applied for several months before working as a state employee, opened up in Gary, Indiana. And, most fortunately of all, ten months later I by chance met my future bride, the mother of our four children. It's a good example of how somewhat opposites can attract. Math was my most difficult subject in both high school and college; and now, I'm happily married to a math teacher.

Getting back to a religious experience, my belief in God stems at least in part from my love of nature. Even as a child, the big vacant lot next door with its small trees, occasional rabbits and abundant insects held my interest. Scouts would sometimes erect a tent there and would show me their boards with various kinds of insects stuck on with straight pins. Not far from our house there was a creek with frogs, turtles, small fish and usually a rope attached to a big tree where one could swing out over the water. I traveled there a lot in the summertime and even went there with my sled in winter when the water was completely frozen. Much later I would make oil paintings of nature scenes, coming at times to the Indiana Dunes to capture its beauty.

How could there be such beauty in nature and in wonderful sunsets if there is no God? Of course, I learned about Charles Darwin and the theory of evolution and his premise that everything started from inert matter that became life in primitive form and then continued to develop into all the plants and animals that we see today.

Personally, I understand the concept but in general I find it a bit hard to believe. However, being an amateur student of science and cosmology, I think about the four inherent forces of nature and how these original forces needed to be present at the beginning of the universe for there to even be a universe. Not only that, but these forces of gravity, electromagnetism, strong force, and weak force are known to have extremely precise values. Any deviation from what scientists have mathematically determined them to be would mean that the Big Bang would not have developed into the universe we know today that allows all life including human beings to exist.

To me, that is proof of the power of our Creator. Without the laws of nature there would be no universe and no life whatever. But perhaps even more significant on a day to day basis is that I feel I can talk to God, with the belief that He cares and listens. One might ask if that can really be the case. Can God actually care about individual people, especially considering that there are so many billions of us? I believe so. I believe He can know each one of us in a personal way.

Though we are all human beings, each of us is different. My belief is that God speaks to each of us as individuals, whether members of a particular church or not. I have confidence in a God with unlimited power. We know that the universe extends out farther than our most powerful telescopes can see and may contain as many as or more than approximately 200 trillion galaxies similar to our own galaxy. Our own Milky Way Galaxy contains approximately 100 billion stars. Not being a mathematician, numbers of this astronomical size are difficult, but findings on the internet come up with a total of 200 billion trillion stars, just in the part of the universe that is visible with the Webb telescope. As the one star that we know well, our own sun, provides the light, warmth, and radiation that makes plants grow and life possible, to me the immense number of suns in just the observable universe demonstrates the unlimited power of our creator. With that in mind, for me there can be nothing too big or difficult for God.

Most people are likely to accept their belief in God on faith alone. It takes no scientific knowledge to feel the presence of God in one's life.

It takes no special skills to feel that one can talk to God and believe that He listens. Christians as well as Muslims and others do it at any time of the day or night. But why would an all powerful God care about human beings? It's a good question, especially as I believe many atheists and others believe He doesn't. Personally, if I didn't have faith, I would also wonder why this all powerful being would have any interest in me or in any of us. His love cannot be because of us or of anything we have done.

My belief is that God's love for us can only be because His nature is love. If God is anything like us at all, He must love what He has created and especially the people He created. His special relationship with people is clearly expressed in Genesis, the first book of the Bible. "So God created man in his own image, in the image of God he created him; male and female he created them." (Genesis 1:27) And again, "Then God said, "Let us make man in our image, after our likeness. And let them have dominion over the fish of the sea and over the birds of the heavens and over the livestock and over all the earth and over every creeping thing that creeps on the earth." (Genesis 1:26)

How do we personally know of God's love? Those who read the Bible are quite familiar with God's relationship with the Jews and later the message of Jesus in the New Testament. The message doesn't always get through to each of us. A famous poem by an opium addicted and often homeless man, Francis Thompson, is titled "Hound of Heaven." A short summary of it is that

God's grace pursues the prodigal human soul until the soul realizes there is nowhere for it to flee except back to God. Thus, according to Thompson's poem, no matter where the soul seeks happiness in the world, it will inevitably be disillusioned unless it finds God.

I personally believe that anyone who wants to find and experience God only needs to take time to listen and be open to God's personal words to each of us. However, God does not touch an unbelieving heart. He doesn't force His way into any person's life. If, as most of us believe, that God created the universe and everything we see in it, then this God is likely to know what will make each of us better off and happier. Nevertheless, we are each given free will and He will not take that away. An individual will need to desire God's presence for God to enter into a relationship with that person.

The Pursuit of Happiness

It is human nature to strive for happiness. However, our happiness can be upset by difficult situations. Sickness, death, divorce, and loss of employment are only a few of the things that human beings may have to contend with at different times in our life. Despite the difficulty, we need to find a way to overcome these personal tragedies as we look forward to better times. There are ways that can be helpful.

We all want happiness and as individuals we pursue happiness in many different ways. Even growing up as young children we enjoy appetizing food. Our taste for what is delicious usually remains with us for the rest of our lives. By the time we reach our teen years, we already have favorite classes, favorite friends and often have already learned special skills at home and away from home. Living in a cosmopolitan world and influenced by incessant media we may learn at an early age about the many life and career choices that are available to us. Still, even today, people often pursue the same or similar vocations as one or the other of their parents.

Then, for most of us, comes the heady fascination we have for members of the opposite sex. From having little use for them as preteens we often come to find them captivating and even alluring. Some years later, the majority of us find love and then marriage, or sex and then marriage or only sex and no marriage.

We look for happiness in our relationships and in our calling, whatever it may be, that will allow us to support ourselves. Hopefully, we will find a job or career to our liking.

Adult years are years of freedom for most of us. We are no longer under the supervision of our parents and once finished with school don't have to be concerned about grades. Adulthood can be a great time of life. Within certain constraints we are free to do what we want to do. Of course, for most of us there is our employment which can be relatively easy or difficult.

As adults we can live our own lives and make our own choices. It is fun to make plans and to decide how we'll use our resources. Will we move from an apartment or condo to a house or from a smaller house to a larger one? If married how many children will we have and will we try to space them or take them as they come. How children will impact our working lives is a consideration most couples will need to think about.

There are so many things we can decide to do as adults. Trips into the country if we live in the city or into the city if we live in the country can be fun and interesting. We can decide where we will go on vacation and, depending on our income, the whole world can be a destination. Or, we can spend some weekends in our own state or local parks enjoying nature and perhaps swimming and hiking.

Our choice of recreation includes all kinds of things including pickle ball, tennis, bike riding, racquetball, camping, and golf, as well as bowling, roller skating, and even adult soccer. Sporting activities are valuable both for socialization and for getting exercise. Cards and board games are also fun to play for both adults and children. Then there's dining at our favorite restaurants, which, if living in a metropolitan area, there are so many choices from Italian, Mexican, American, Greek, Indian, Asian and so many others. It's also good for couples to get out on their own at times even if it means having to pay a babysitter. Whatever our choices in life, and we have so many, psychologists and others tell us that enjoying <u>experiences</u> in life brings far more happiness than making expensive purchases.

Human beings are by nature social. We are stimulated in the presence of others. We need to make time for getting together with friends and family. Spending time together enjoying simple meals like burgers, pizza or chicken or at other times for significant events like weddings, birthdays, baptisms, and major anniversaries is important and often quite memorable.

For most of us who are not well off there is the issue of money. Buying a Porsche or Maserati on a Chevy or Ford budget is a recipe for financial difficulty. Pickup trucks are often fascinating to men, with their power, size and capabilities. Unfortunately, a full size one costs considerably more than most cars and if fully equipped even more than luxury cars. Similarly, financing the purchase of a mini mansion with an average income can also be a bit daunting. We all face a constant stream of advertising, most of it telling us how our lives will be better if we buy various products. Advertisers are smart, they know how to use imagery and psychology to weaken our natural defenses that tell us we don't need or can't afford the product.

We all have to live within our means. Personally speaking, with four young children and one parent working we needed to economize. Early on we made a rule for ourselves that anything we bought on credit we would pay for that month rather than incur the huge interest that credit cards charge on the unpaid balance. Things were tight but I looked at the big picture. Living in America on our budget we were better off than 85 to 90% of the people in the rest of the world. Of course, once my wife returned to work, things were much easier, at least until it was time to pay for college educations.

Unfortunately, life throws us curves or we create them for ourselves. Life can become difficult, even messy. Being fired or laid off from a job, a major sickness of ourself or someone we love, and even getting a promotion can sometimes make life more difficult, especially if a promotion means having to move to another city. None of these things are easy, in particular in the exceptional situation when a family member or a child is significantly handicapped or facing death. We often just don't know or understand how to deal with these kinds of calamities.

Then, there are the personal situations. What if the marriage is not working out? What does one do? There are many temptations in life. What if you or your partner are finding love in the arms of another? Infidelity is nothing new in the history of mankind. The vow to love one another "till death do us part" sometimes doesn't seem to have a lot of meaning. Unfortunately, at the very least, a marriage breakup ordinarily brings difficult situations for everyone involved including any children.

Yes, life can be difficult. Just keeping up with the news can be disconcerting. Many years ago, my dentist said he didn't read the newspaper—too depressing. Today we can very easily have the same experience watching the news on TV. Add to that a life busy with cares and responsibilities, it's no wonder people can become depressed. I think it's important to take time each day to de-stress. There are many suggestions on how to do this. A few are getting some exercise including taking a walk, meditating, and writing down our thoughts in a personal journal. Others are mindful breathing, playing or listening to music, and calling to mind people and things we are grateful for. For me, prayer, especially at the end of the day is calming.

Faith can help. God knows our human weaknesses. Yes, He wants us to get things right as best we can. He wants us to forgive, and if possible, to make amends. He knows all of our human imperfections. Yet he still loves us. In the case of sickness and death, knowing that they are a part of human existence since the beginning of time may help to put our own personal tragedies in some perspective. Having a spouse or friendships that stand by us in difficult times is a huge asset for dealing with and overcoming the major upsets in life.

Some individuals and families are able to handle the difficulties of life. Other families break apart, each blaming the other(s) for what may have possibly been no one's fault. Some turn away from God, blaming Him for their personal tragedies.

However, aside from unexpected adversities, we typically look forward to lives of happiness. We try to make the most of our own personal situations as best as we can. It's an emotionally healthy way to live. We all have our own individual talents, things that we are good at.

Ideally, we should be recognized for our successes in life no matter what they are. We should also be thankful that we have these God given personal talents.

Medical assistance may at times be necessary to help deal with particularly stressful situations. More people today are prescribed medications for dealing with anxiety than at any other time in our history. It's a stressful world, and often we don't take the time or have the time to deal with life's issues. If pills are what it takes to achieve wellbeing, then maybe it is the right choice.

One well known strategy for helping to relieve our concerns and doldrums is philanthropy. Donating to worthwhile causes to help those less fortunate helps each of us to remember there are many who are worse off than we are. If time permits, actually volunteering at food kitchens, pantries, shelters, etc. helps to put our own needs in perspective. Frequently, doing so also leads to new friendships. In everything, being grateful for what we have as well as for our family and friends is key to a happier life.

Non-Prayers and Prayers, from Atheist to Christian

The first of these could be called a non-prayer, which an atheist might prefer. Consider this: if one's parents have both died, would it be of any value to write a letter to one or both of them? I think so. Even for those who don't believe in an afterlife, the act of addressing our own important thoughts on any particular subject may be valuable for us.

Atheist: I have a brain and am able to distinguish between truth and falsehood. I am glad to be able to use my intellect to determine the best course for my life. I see all around me people who believe in superstition and angels and devils. I see no sign of any of that, but know that others have a long history of ascribing importance to invisible beings. I have no need for what is called spirituality. If I am missing out on anything then it my own fault in lacking perception. I strive to understand things on my own without the need for immaterial beings. If I should possibly be wrong in my lack of belief, then enlighten me if you can. And, if there really is a spirit in the sky, I think you need to show me something to make me a believer.

Agnostic: I really don't know if there is a god or not. In a way, I'd like to think there is. It really would be good if there was a God who actually cared about individuals. Unfortunately, such a God who cared about some and not about others would be unfair and I can't see that kind of God anyway. I pray for understanding and contentment in life for myself and also that the less fortunate get a break. That, by the way, is another reason I have my doubts about God. There is so much misery and suffering in the world. Can't you fix that, God? Anyway, if you are really out there, let me know. I could personally use a little help, and if you are God, you know how to answer my thoughts.

Deist: I honor you, the God of the heavens. You must have been present in the creation of this wonderful universe. I don't know if there is anything else you need to do as everything seems to be in place, the stars, sun, earth and moon, etc. Anyway, I can't imagine how you could take an interest in the lives of us billions of individuals each with our own wishes and desires. It's enough that you created this system that keeps everything going from day to day and from year to year. I really can't imagine you as a personal god concerned about all of us, young and old and everyone in between of every race, nationality and color. You've given us a pretty good world, not perfect, and it's up to us to try to make it better for all.

Christian: The **Lord's Prayer** as Christ taught to the apostles.

Our Father, who art in heaven, hollowed be thy name. Thy kingdom come, thy will be done on earth as it is in heaven. Give us this day, our daily bread and forgive us our trespasses as we forgive those who trespass against us. Lead us not into temptation but deliver us from evil. Amen.

Catholic Christians also usually know the Hail Mary prayer and the Glory Be:

Glory be to the Father, to the Son and to the Holy Spirit, as it was in the beginning is now and ever shall be world without end. Amen.

A favorite Christian Prayer is this one attributed to St. Francis of Assisi.

Lord, make me an instrument of your peace,

where there is hatred, let me sow love;

where there is injury, pardon;

where there is doubt, faith

where there is despair, hope;

where there is darkness, light;

where there is sadness, joy.

O divine Master, grant that I may not so much seek
to be consoled as to console,

to be understood as to understand,

to be loved as to love.

For it is in giving that we receive,

it is in pardoning that we are pardoned,

and it is in dying that we are born to eternal life.

Amen.

The Jewish Shema prayer

[Considered by many Jews to be the most
important prayer in Judaism.]

"Hear, O Israel, the Lord is our God, the Lord is
one. And as for you, you shall love the Lord your
God with all of your heart, with all your soul, and
with all your strength."

Books That May Interest You

The Bible: There is so much inspiration in both the old and new Testaments! Of the four Gospel accounts, Luke may be the easiest to start with. Of the Bible's 150 psalms, one can choose between many that address all kinds of life situations as well as giving praise to God. For intimate, joyous human love read the **Song of Songs**. Unfortunately, it's not included in most Protestant Bibles but it is available online.

Your God is too Small: This short, timeless classic by J.B. Phillips describes common mistaken notions of God and then does a good job of describing the real nature of God and Jesus Christ.

Jesus > Religion: Why He is So Much Better than Trying Harder, Doing More, and Being Good Enough: Youthful author Jeff Bethke made a huge hit on You Tube with his passionate poem, **"Why I Hate Religion but Love Jesus."** His book is an Amazon bestseller. It is open, candid and personal.

The Case for a Creator: One of many short books by Lee Strobel, in this one the journalist investigates scientific evidence that points directly to the universe having been created by a loving God. The science in this book may be easier to understand than most books on the subject.

God, The Evidence: By Patrick Glynn. The book's subtitle is, The Reconciliation of Faith and

Reason in a Postsecular World. This book, more than any other, for me covers all the bases from atheism, Darwinism, the universe, psychology, religion, health and near death experiences.

How Christianity Changed the World: Alvin Schmidt's book of over 400 pages details the tremendous impact Christianity has had on life throughout the ages. It details how Christianity ended crucifixions and infanticide, and opened the first hospitals for the general public, promoted education, fostered science, and was a major contributor to art and architecture. From the early medieval days to the Renaissance and beyond, the world would be a far different place today without the impact of Christianity.

The Reason for God, subtitled, Belief in an Age of Skepticism. Written by Timothy Keller, who before his death was the pastor of a large Presbyterian Church in Manhattan. A very well written and personal approach to answering most of the reasons people have for rejecting Christianity.

Return of the God Hypothesis, subtitled Three Scientific Discoveries that Reveal the Mind Behind the Universe. This book is by Stephen Meyer, a well known scientist. It is 500 pages of rather scientific language contending against other scientists of our day who reject God. Not an easy read, however he brings together recent scientific findings and comes to the conclusion that the creator of the universe is a personal God.

Books, Nonfiction and Fiction by the Author

Mary, the Girl Who Said Yes

Mary, the mother of Jesus, was a young girl when asked by the angel to be Christ's mother. When she answered yes, she could not have known all that would then happen. That her son would be born in a shelter for animals, that she and Joseph would have to flee a murderous king, and that Jesus' life would be far from glorious and would end on a cross.

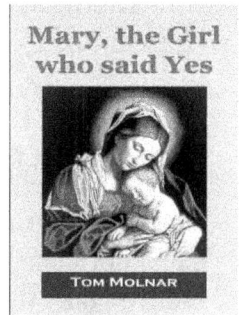

Mary's story is one of danger and excitement, love, sorrow and uncertainty. Delving into her life as seen in the Gospels shows her to be a spirited and courageous woman, a fitting mother for Jesus, and an inspiration for us all.

A book praised by a bishop, a priest, and a book reviewer.

Swept Away

Swept Away draws from Civil War records, from accounts of life in the times, and from a true love story. It brings to life the story of Jenny, a girl turning 18 as the war begins. It finds her caught up in the love of a man for whom she is only his "best friend."

When Daniel leaves to fight for the South, Jenny's small town and her father's farm are soon occupied by hated Yankee soldiers. One of them, a Union captain, has the audacity to smile at her.

As the war intensifies, Jenny will find courage to do things she never thought she would do, and she will see things she never thought she would see.

Swept Away brings home the reality of war as well as life as it was lived in rural America. It is Jenny's story, one of love, the unexpected, and beginning anew.

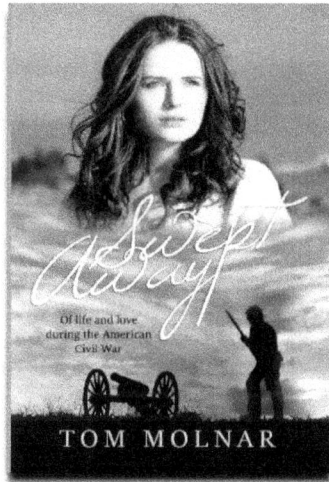

Dark Age Maiden

Lady Carina has boldly told her father, lord of the Manor, that she will not marry the man he has chosen for her. Soon, she comes to know the power of love. But is it too late? Enemies assail the fortress, where her family, knights, and peasants fight to keep them out. Their horses and cattle have already been stolen leaving them little chance to escape.

95

Slipping out before dawn, Carina rushes toward the deep forest, hoping to reach the powerful dark knight her father told her about. Unknown to her, there is someone else she will meet in the woods. . .

Dark Age Woman *(sequel to Dark Age Maiden)*

Carina hopes at last to find happiness with her brave knight. Then, tragically, he falls in battle. When he comes back to her, he is a changed man. Can he once again become the valiant, strong and loving knight who has somehow found a way to win her intrepid heart?

Carina vows to win him back, completely. She will do whatever it takes to rekindle the fire of their love. Meanwhile, danger threatens. Too soon, the vast army of the enemy appears outside the walls of the city. Must they give them what they want to save their lives?

Recent Nonfiction

Jesus, Kind, Loving, Dangerous

The Pharisees realized right away that Jesus was a dangerous man. He was breaking their religious laws and keeping company with sinners. Ultimately, they had him crucified.

We, however, often get the watered down version of Jesus depicted in books and movies. He doesn't seem dangerous to us, but he is. His life changing message is not one of following laws, but of transforming hearts.

JESUS
KIND, LOVING,
DANGEROUS
Tom Molnar

Not everyone grows up in a happy home with loving parents. I didn't. Today, most of us don't experience enough happiness in our daily lives. Anyone can feel downhearted. The key is knowing the ways to overcome our sadness.

Increasing happiness is much easier if we know how. Unfortunately, many of the ways commonly thought to bring happiness are wrong. This is proven by observation as well as by scientific studies.

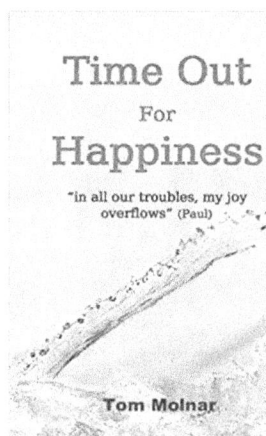

Time Out
For
Happiness

"in all our troubles, my joy overflows" (Paul)

Tom Molnar

Time Out for Happiness delivers insightful thinking on how to minimize sadness and increase joy. It features quick pick me ups as well as longer term strategies. Once we discard the ways that don't bring happiness and focus on those that do, like sharing with others, we will be well on our way to living a happier life. The truths found in this book are affirmed by those who have spent much of their working lives finding real answers to what brings happiness and joy.

The Universe of God and Humanity

Start with Adam and Eve and add evolution—two different stories or do they come together? Then add the discoveries that even Einstein couldn't believe, ones that have now quietly become a fact of life. Discoveries that have the power to change our view of God and the universe.

Already, the unexpected power of quantum mechanics is being used in our everyday lives, in cell phones, in lasers and at store checkout counters. What are the strange qualities of matter that can change how we look not only at the universe but also God and creation?

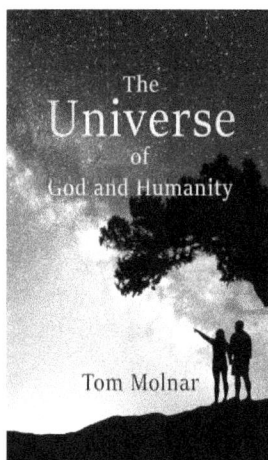

The
Universe
of
God and Humanity

Tom Molnar

Let's start at the beginning, in the world we thought we knew, but one whose true nature is far different than we realized. A world where the unexpected happens every day.

Also available as a .99 cent eBook

Wired for Love

We all need love, from the strongest man to the most delicate woman. Young children, without love, are likely to die. All evidence shows that we human beings are genetically "hard wired" to give and receive love. In its absence, studies show that we tend to die sooner and experience far less happiness in our lives.

Our "attachment style," affects how we love and whom we love, and even those with whom we find it easiest to get along. Now, we are able to learn our own attachment style and that of our partner. The bonus is that in doing so we are likely build our esteem and increase our happiness as well as the happiness of the one we love.

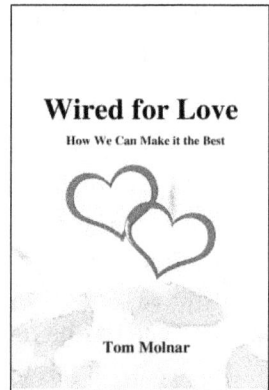

Wired for Love
How We Can Make it the Best

Tom Molnar

All titles are available on Amazon

The Crisis of Christianity
The Turning Point

Why have people walked away from church? Why do many children of faith-filled parents not attend services? Why do many parents today feel the need to protect their children from the negative influences of society?

Though we live in a time of change, surveys show that most people still believe in God. Even those who seldom or never attend religious services often maintain some prayer life and devotion. Nevertheless, it is undeniable that in Europe and much of the United States churches are closing and the number of Christians attending services is declining.

Why? This book will describe what has been happening in our culture and in our lives that has turned many away from their religious heritage. And yet, going forward, there is hope for the future.

Coming Soon

Mist on the Moon

An adventurous love story

Unfortunately, as the daughter of a lord, she knows she can't marry just anyone. No, the peasants in her kingdom can wed for love, lucky them, but Cara needs to marry someone to form an alliance against the enemy. The enemy that is threatening Europe.

Cara understands. She knows she may be paired with a man twice her age or even with a tyrant. Thinking about the distressing prospect, her thoughts turn to another. Though beneath her in rank, there is something in his eyes when he looks at her. She should pay him no mind. There is no way she can know what is coming.

All titles are available on Amazon. This one soon.